Goodnight Mr Moo

Writ-en & Illustrated by

Liberty Aldridge

ISBN: 9781838092320

For my brothers
Callum & Jude

Once there lived a handsome young boy called Jude.

One day he decided to go for a walk to see the moos

while he was walking down the road, he saw a horse.

Jude said "Goodnight Mr Horse"

Then he walked some more and found a sheep.

Jude said "Goodnight Mr Sheep"

Then he walked some more and saw a tortoise.

Jude said "Goodnight Mr Tortoise"

Then he walked some more and saw some birds.

Jude said "Goodnight Mr Bird"

Then he walked some more and found a monkey.

Jude said "Goodnight Mr Monkey"

Then he walked some more and found a peacock.

Jude said "Goodnight Mr Peacock"

Then he walked some more and found the Moos

Jude said "Goodnight Mr Moo"

Then on his way home to bed he thought of all the animals he had seen on his walk.

The End

www.ingramcontent.com/pod-product-compliance
Lightning Source LLC
Chambersburg PA
CBHW040023050426

42452CB00002B/105